LONE PINE

NORTH WOODS

LONE PINE

NORTH WOODS

JAMESON KOOPER

MISCHIEVOUS BOOKS

www.mischievousbooks.com
CALGARY, CANADA

Cover Design, Editing, Layout
Brenda Fisk

Library and Archives Canada Cataloguing in Publication

Kooper, Jameson, author
     Lone pine : north woods / Jameson Kooper

Poems.
Issued in print and electronic formats.
ISBN 978-0-9939823-5-4 (softcover).--ISBN 978-0-9939823-6-1 (ebook).--
ISBN 978-0-9939823-7-8 (EPUB)

     I. Title.

PS8621.O656L66 2016   C811'.6   C2016-907960-0
                                              C2016-907961-9

DEDICATION

Writing poetry is always a surprise. I never know what they will become until they finalize like ice before me. I find them after reading Shakespeare. I find them when walking through crowded pavilions. I find them when I sit quietly looking at former buildings across a street from a mall bench. I find them as I work a tune that won't leave my mind. Poets have given me inspiration. Lewis Carrol, with his nonsense rhymes has forever played muse. Leonard Cohen's lyric craft has sparked my own attempts to write to chords and notes. Ancient texts influence the spare quality of my odes. Few will have read Gilgamesh, the ancient search for life everlasting. But his struggle to find meaning in life informs my poetry often giving these little pieces purpose. Finally where ever I have trod, whether it is in the backyard of my home where balsam fir and white spruce rail against wind or on an expressway south of Brandon, Manitoba, where coyotes sing and northern lights play, our wonderful planet guides my muse because wonder at life has that way with us all. The daily struggle of living that one sees in nature translates to me: struggling daily as I do to understand, and figure out my place in the Universe wide. This is why these poems first found light in day. Because when the dark tries to claim me, light breaks from within shattering to splinters this mirror that attempts to rend my soul to ruin. It is in those moments of supreme doubt, anger, spit and vengeance that I find my voice. And it is this light that springs it free to the page for others to read. Sometimes I even find clarity. I hope you the reader will enjoy these simple spare verses. I hope you will identify your own dark place and find a way that guides to the light. For the light is always warm. The light always springs songs of life. It is in the light that we gain wisdom.

CONTENTS

ACKNOWLEDGMENTS

To Angela and Henry Kooper who spent a lifetime trying
to figure me out and help me through the rough days
and to Brenda Fisk, who has given these little odes a
chance to breathe fresh and fly free.

AUTHOR'S PREFACE

I have always been a writer.

Not one of those internet types

leaving anonymous notes to all the passing fauna

nor the card dealer

pulling teeth so the music is sickly sweet for all seasons

a Hallmark second.

I am not even the bloated beast

that "writer" conjures, autographs

and bestsellers, or even a chapbook of

published moments.

In better times or maybe worse,

I am what I always was;

paper and pen tagging along like a

cat I once knew

curling up behind,

waiting for the first ink

to fall,

mellow reeds sung

and rambles of riving toiling

out from confused fingers.

I have always been a writer

just a simple stroke in a mall corridor

where no one else notices.

I

LIGHT

THE LONE PINE

There she stands,
Wounded by time,
Great boughs reaching
To catch noon-day sun.

In queenly green robes
She stands above
Boughs of spruce,
Majestic like liberty,
Her torch whispering needles
Embedded by breeze.

I hear she brooks
No folly though below
River cascades
Towards that far distant
Land of rock and dirt
That once called the world
Beautiful.

Some wolves are careful
To rest in shade by
Tangled roots
For like all God's creatures
They are open to death,
The kingmaker,
That final brokered truce.

Even deer that nip at
Moss and leaf litter
Seem reticent of that
Dark space below branches.

She has lived and ached
Through every storm
Held the snow so deep
Wood cracked from
Heavy lifting.

Yet her trunk back
Holds unsmitten by firelight
Flung from angry storms.

For survivors are like that
Able to hold fast to earth
Where others fall
Broken to the needle strewn
Soil.

December 11, 2015

GOD'S MOUNTAINTOP

When sun rose past crest of hill and pine,
each poplar leaf, each birch bough shook
with jewels,
a green sea shimmering as each moment
passed; each branch blessed by dew.

I smiled cradled in your moss arms;
soaped each sud of sun with eyes closed
and
touched your warm glow with my skin.

I felt your caress slowly engulf mine
until I cried bless thyself over and over in
echoes
knowing each distant cloud was your
smile
returned.

June 20, 1992

GARTER SNAKE

How silent

I have become

Watching garters

Sun along

Cement, God's ancient nemesis

So I hear.

Slithering to find

The hot

Spot among shales

And granites

That keep water out

They taste air.

I'll wager they

Know I stand feet away

The next gen over

From the asteroid

That tore a world

And breathed new life

Into smaller things.

They inherit grass
Full with ants fleeing
With giant morsels
For their nest.

They prowl roots where
Toads shade and mice
Peek to seek fresh greens.

Slow, the surprise
Of fangs catch quick the
Little worm that flails
In death.

Soundless as atoms
They lie again
Reaping glowing
Sun, warming blood to prowl again.

November 15, 2016

SUMMER MILK

I saw the ancient light,

beacons

blinking

from distant mists of milky way

home of lives

seeking

high

the hope of rocky

worlds

basking

in glow.

I hear these

tenuous fires that warm

the cloud

sprinkle sparkles upon

deep blue oceans,

feed green shoots, bring new strength

to fill galaxy arms

in blue youth!

Strange, dark matter,
filling void and pulling
light apart should
attempt the
toppling of
stars
and force ancient storms
to snuff like candles.

Yet, misty milky arms seethe
against the coming dark
that promises cold and
death.

Strange that these ancient
souls that wink
and build might
one day
leave a sky
black and lost.
October 24, 2016

HYMN

You are my bright red tulip but unlike

others in brim fat vases

you never fade, never wither into aged

purple on the vine

but

continue day upon day breathing deep the

fresh clear liquid,

beneath your

strong taut stem,

blooming pride

on my window sill and by my bedside

candle.

Summer 1992

UNSURE

Amazing!

I could sing such
silly rhymes beneath
my breath all those years
past, when memory was
present and future was
waiting.

They came like drizzle,
faint,
barely noticeable.

They were gay
as if they had never met with
gloom.

I praised Allah
Yaweh, Christ
Vishnu
as if they were just glinting

steel.

I danced the fool
in front of the entire class
of peers because love was fresh in the
afternoon.

I sang as sparrows do
or loons at midnight
haunting malls with tunes
of sweetness,
new
freshness
just arrived.

How I felt graceful
in yonder days,
a king of happy.

I was
never aware how sad it all
could turn
how sudden I could

grow limbs I didn't
need

turn trees of birch and cedar
into smoking cinders
freshly licked by fires
of distain.

I never thought I could spit
Allah Yaweh, Vishnu, Christ
with venom only asps can when rustled
awake
or turn from my class of peers
to hide among the sands
of some hellish lake.

How I long to be
King of happy again.

How I wish I could
dance and haunt malls with music.

How I
dream of days

when I built up stories instead of
tearing them down.

How I kept vigil over my
seeds of birch.

1992

QUETICO PARK
LOGGING ROAD

In writing for trees,

the script calls for balsam fir,

their soft boughs raising trunks into

spearheads that gouge cloud above.

They master wind currents. Sailors of

earth ships they steer air down paths and

crannies into fern oceans and cherry

islands.

I made the white pine queen, the black

spruce her squires, but the editor would

not hear of it.

So I heeded her word, seeded bald patches

of hill with long pine cones so that lakes

would grow majestic in their reach.

Thrones I built of granite and shale,

adorned each with lichen flats and moss

beds so their trunks rested, peace
disturbed by flitters of bird song, dull
collapse of bear returned like juice to soil.

I know the script is long on spruce, devoid
of birch but it is alive with green, the light
filtering down the cracks of forest to rest
where saws take over.

August 30, 1993

THE LOON

In fog he sat,

lone mandarin of lake beds,

the call

a song ghosts sing when the water

is lapping rocks.

He waited to hear

the answer to his prayer

as the pine loomed so

but none came.

Midnight answers no one.

1993

WILD FIRE AT FORT MAC

The creeping thing comes,
Quiet at first,
Hardly noticeable like drops in dry
Puddle tracks.

But feasts are
Quick
Sudden
Rich in orange
Flashing clouds
As the great maw consumes,
Ever growing, to meet
Fresh food.

The cloak of Darth
Climbs to choke
The sun
Creating its own
World.

Jumping Flash and Cement wilts,

Passed by for propane

And gas chews

hors d'oeuvres

I hear.

This is sugar that feeds flickering

Flames

Wine toasted as structure

Crumbles in death

Ruins of 40 years, only

So much smoke in a night

But it is not done!

Cheerleading breeze

Guides like a blind-man's pet

Casting new tracks

New hurdles

New grass to fete a

hungry hot belly.

This is

Frankenstein crossing

The river
To taste tender shoots on
The other side
The swings and things
Of past lives
Leaving faded soot
And broken pipes spewing water
Left on.

I hear there are many ways
To fight leviathans.

Forceful sprays,
Breaks to build black
Earth
Starving the thing it is hoped.

But disturbed ant hills
Take time to group
Though time is quickly shed
By this king
Of beasts.
It takes time

To deprive
Feasts of delicacies.

I hear drenching rains
Can change battles
And win wars
Welcome cool can weaken
Flickering arms, take muscle out
Of jumping light.

I hear with the right
Conditions
Hunger can be sated
Feast finished
Leaving smoldering
Ash
Broken buildings
The skeletons of Hondas
Left on work paths long ago.

I hear
With the right conditions
Peace

Can be restored to the valley

In singed golden arches

So that ants can set to

Work before the winter comes.

May 5, 2016

THE TERRITORIAL BEAST

Wake me slow

for

the ease

of robin's song

fills

the birch

with restless branches.

I hear them call, making love,

I understand,

their challenges

met

with angry shrills.

Curious how we,

among shapes and concrete

have moved beyond calls

and chirps

meant to defy

the suitor.

How quick we lose

sense,

that the ISIL beast

is just another bird

challenging the nest

strafing the ground

to take it for its own.

How far

we have gone

only to find fallow

earth before us.

April 2015

SOFT AS WOOD

They have all found their promised lands
simple as wind.

Full with babies, careers, wives,
husbands,
they have found the soft quilt of life
as gratifying as new found snow nestled
upon quiet boughs after storms have
passed.

I should envy I suppose
shut up like a kite
inside a cupboard place,
collapsed wood and rigging
surviving the swift crests
that topple boats into brine.

Stranger to a quiet sea I have never found
promised ground rich in shrubs,
worms turning the compost nutrients,

mixing the

land and making it whole.

Never have I seen the light I suppose

like so many others who met and held

gentle hand,

sniffed the scent of love deep

as permafrost.

I figure I grew strange as a TARDIS

traveller

passing through

always passing through.

Incessant I suppose.

Ah me! Survivor as I knock

(never know

what wind may finally cut rigging apart),

Still trapped in my home so past

where youth spins tales,

love conquers fish,

and cats, careful, jump upon silent

jay.

Happy hermitage, grand as death
quiet as twisting flakes white
I still have a place.

Just can't make out the title.

November 22, 2015

THE MIND MARSH

Once upon
Midday heat
My thoughts did flounder to
The pit, dank like musk,
Loose and lost.
Yea I knew the better path like any
Good natured bloke,
The line of birch and pine.

An
Eager wind did blow
Forth towards cavalry,
But as always I took
This flow of
Curled and broken aspen,
Tortured by funnel clouds,
Towards the marsh of despond,

This land That catches.
Yea I found this home,

Ooze splattering
The glade in muck,
Sinking thoughts into quicksand
To die.
Few find sanctuary far from these
Unsettled banks,

For placid waters do not a marsh make.
Rather here I wallowed
Avoiding flies with thick ooze to cover,
Seeking sustenance from wilted cat tails
Lining the shore.
Here my soul sank into the dusk
Of death imprinted in its ornate trappings,
The eaglet mounted to catch tender fish.

My mind would mine:
A leopard frog slinking slowly to take down
Each fly my mind could make.
Yea here I lay, torpid, reduced
To a tortured animal wounded by
Angry eyes,
Each thought a morsel for the next

Predator.

I am my own worst enemy:
Mind ready to swim waist deep
In this blackened land
rather than climb banks
And saunter to finer fields
Where pine and birch
Blow and sway
To the song of glory.

June 16, 2016

ALONE WITH MY SHADOW

Ah shade
following along through every crevasse!
How well-worn your path should be.

Are you some manifestation of God
set here like shackles
binding me to this piece of earth?

Strange how well you face the light
streaming through glass
panes

uninterrupted till broken by
my. . . well
yes, I suppose I grew some girth

for you to frolic with, growing long
in lamplight
short in close.

You would think I found some crazy

mirror
for you to streak through.

Ah shade
friend of the dark
the place skeletons go
when closets fill.

I hear you keep track of all those
failures past when pines were supple
young things just finding roots.

Sometimes I can even hear you
traipse those tales when life seemed
promise ridden
and I the dutiful slave to disappointment.

Strange old friend passing by the car port
young
how you have crossed heaven and earth
without reaching sky.
how you wander so like incessant
wind,

buffeting roof edge.

Ah shade
will you follow along
when Hades
calls
or secrete new
paths along bitter trails,
crazed old fiend you are,

King of the grass
yet unable to grasp fronds.

Strange old partner
you are my friend
strange, distant,
dark.

November 23, 2015

MADNESS

Since when do we

Strike the black bear

Down

For

Stumbling

Past the garden fair

Towards woods

Safe with roots

And berries?

Do we not see he lumbers away

Innocent

Of blood

Spilled in street before.

Can we not see he

Tries to survive

Life like all,

Catching fish spawning upstream

Away

From the circus tents below?

Can we not see he is just another
Part of nature's fabric
That sweet grass of eagle
And crow singing out
To compliment the breeze?

Can we not see he poses
No threat for lumbering by
Ignoring carrots ripe with green stalks?

Can we not find a new nirvana
Where fur is just soft
Goodness lying by a pillow somewhere
Rather than bludgeoned red by stupidity
Unleashed?

July 10, 2016

II

DUSK

OCTOBER

Colour melting,

Naked the branches

Flail

Against bitter October's gales.

I hear the eagle masters wind currents

To spring fear

Among the rabble;

The squirrel wrestling cones from broken

Pine needles;

The bear listless to find

Sleeping quarters.

Only does and fawns

Roam together

To nip at wilted violet stems,

A left over blade of grass

In rebellious green

As if to taunt October grace.

Yes, as life shuts up,
The dull cocoon awaiting time
When snow will rule
This world of
Drab,
I often wonder why
death
Must be so blatant.

Why must this world of
Bucks and does
Succumb to November fists
Full with bladeless
Snow lawns?

Why must life hide behind
Curtains
Made cold
By hoar frost
Fronds?

Why must bitter
Breezes

Turn a once fed

Field into fallow

Twigs and

Naked birch trunks?

Why must October life die

To renew a world

Covered in November snow?

October 10, 2015

SLOUGH OF DESPOND

Slough, that catches and holds feet fast
Like muck should, swallowing my form
Like a quiet beast cold;
I should struggle but I hear sinking.

Feelings come faster the more
You fight and flinch.
Perhaps I should catch on to branch and
Hold
Tight.

But branches snap the moment pulled,
And torn loose
Lay limp in hand.

Perhaps a smile or two from passersby
Will relieve burden gained.

But nowadays they run frightened from
The field

For fear of bomb blasts and shaken
Buildings.

O slough in field that saps my strength
And sings me to dark sleep
Why can you not bend rules once
And allow for better days?

September 6, 2016

COSMIC STRING

Where have you gone my cosmic string,
cosmic bang?

Were you meant to leave a trace in the sea
of stars
the ocean of galaxies that still move on
drifting along
like yo-yo pieces, twirling?

I could watch from Epsilon Eridani and
still see you there
like so many others have seen, black,
empty, the hollow
that God truly is.

You know maybe it isn't I who suffers
mania;
perhaps I am just a piece of God's dust
after all
for like that great empty space

so am I;

like the ocean of darkness

so am I.

45

Perhaps I was created after all to relieve

the manias of greater things.

November 26, 1993

ATIKOKAN

Ah! Blue sky still

embraces,

lush with

cotton curd

though somewhere

these park lands

seem to hush

into silence

as I tread by.

Do not know

what it is

about this old mining

hovel

keeping tune with

bracing breeze.

Seems we are separate

one here and now,

the other a ghost

refused passage to
finer shores.

I ask what have I done
to make
this hamlet,
full
of Steep Rock tomes
and Pluswood riches,
forsake
a former son.

Perhaps
I am clustered with lesions,
the leper reduced
to tormented skin
that no soul dare touch.

Some days it feels as
though resumes are scratch,
a book of dead no one can fathom.
Ah! How my mind plays
its sadist role:

A model
I suppose that still
haunts from childhood
when taunts were king
and I was loyal subject.
Never found a seat at court
then.

Closet dark, I dangled,
safe, among Sound of Music
repeats, honing my instrument
till it glistened like fine wine,
a blues voice sharpened by
uni visits with Mama Rainey.

Then was then, when torment
rained as apples, all my own making,
A connoisseur who learned how to bake
pity pie and suicide shakes,
terrible flavours concocted from roots
of hell.

But away from frog song

and loon call,
I did find city scape howling coyote
melancholy and pining prairie dog,
Blue mountains like haze,
a sky stretching as far as God could make.

Somehow I found a partner willing,
a place to call mine.
Print shop fast, flying free, I could
make my way uncluttered, at least, by
some of those
trappings
death might bring.

Ah those days when I felt like king over
the
apple orchard,
they pass like gas
leaving traces to sputter the sky.
Now we dance again, you and I.

Some days feels like divorce court,
the savage friend turned foe

lashing at my wounded sides,

slinking about,

offering a tender morsel

only to dash it upon the ground

as abrupt as news.

Other days, deer encroach,

welcome visitors, reminding

me I am after all one of God's strange little

creatures,

a wonder of birth,

a Davros of death.

Ah how the mind tricks.

I know how chess is played

but never the player.

Checkmate is hard to grasp

when pieces fail to fall

in place.

December 4, 2015

EPIPHANY

When looking

Towards

Greying fluff

I realize beyond

Bull lies real truth;

That high above

Lies speckled space,

Galaxies cluttered

In colour,

Empty time

Far beyond telescope

Reach where

Cosmic radiation

Explains stars.

How easy to seek

Guidance from a

Solitary being

Clouded in invisible ink

When beyond
Lies the feckless
Sky
Spilling its secrets
In shade and light.

Once in distant
Memory I felt
A mountain top
Where bliss was God
And all things were possible.

Fool I was to believe
When reality spoke
Loudly of big bangs, crackling
A universe free
And sending shards to make
Wind and rain.

How I should have listened
To truth before me
Rather than to seek guidance
In strange prattling of a useless sage.

Ah me!

I think I have come home.

February 6, 2016

PORTRAIT OF AGE

Grey,
There are signs
That steel is melting
To slag.

I see it sitting in comfy
Chair
Peering
Through windows of the past;

I see it trying to stand,
Trip, stand
And hobble
Towards
Kitchen sink
Indomitable of spirit
Yet sinking in strength.

I hear there are ways to
Build a better tram

To pass through this way.
But age is a chain
Grown from links and locks
Holding down the good soul
Weakening each struggling
Heart beat.

I see time
Coming
To catch
You from your roost.

I see steel melting to slag
The final resting place of all.

May 5, 2016

MOM AS SHE AGES

I feel her
Slipping away
Like a fish
Sliding from dock wood
To the murky world below.

She has been such
A spark of light
Blinding breeze
And tree and wave.

Sharp as prairie wind
Diced cold by winter's charms
She seems in spring
To be withering on the vine.
The flower has not come.
The buds do not break.
The lake does not sow new green.

She seems to be

Dying

Away

An ember of that brighter before,

When this pond was the castle of

Blue frequented by loon and bear

Where herons waded to catch

Flittering fish

In noon day sun.

But spring lies

Dormant.

Bird song hides in broken branches

And blue is a brackish brown

And sky, woven purple, signals

star time to come.

How I fear this moment

When she moves toward

Death

I fear this moment when the ghost

Comes to roost.

April 26, 2016

CORONARY GLOW

I sense

Twilight's last gleaming:

A heart shattered

By fool's gold

Thrown by idle hand.

Ah! This rush of fall

That has settled upon

Red cells pumping

To ancient songs.

How did it come to this?

Leaves settling upon

Valves and arteries

Clogging veins until

Strokes

Break through to conquer spirit.

I have heard it said there is still time

To rake the muck

And bag the leaves
That make a heart a withered
Thing;

Run the mile,
Swim the lake.
But oh how cold
The autumn
Gales that
Warn of impending snow.

How can one grow beyond
When white death comes
To claim the soil
And cover
Over the remaining soul
Left listless by
The evening glow?

October 28, 2016

CLIMATE CHANGE

I sense dust
Has yet to settle
Upon windy
Way,

A path travelled
By fiends and furies
That beg
Indulgence this
Bitter day.

November rains
Threaten
Freezing
Folly and drown
Snows of yesteryear
Melting blankets meant
For dead leaves and sleeping things.

Is this climate change

Hated paragon

Of ancient days?

Am I witness to the turning of

The torch?

Are these pouring

Tears from grey above

Just surprise from

One brief

Storm,

A phantom of God's imagination?

Do Chinese seed clouds to keep

Me up at night wondering if

The page is turning

On nature's soul?

November 28, 2016

III

DARKNESS

TANNENBAUM

When every branch

Covered

Lies a statue to the breeze,

I think how

Glass can easily break

If jostled

Quick and fast.

Ah queen pine you are a sight,

Those nimble needles

Held

By space

The foul fiend that

Gravity has yet to settle.

I see needle wheat grasp sky

As if this too belongs in wayward green.

Reach for sun

To melt the white cloak

Donned for this day

Or restless throw it off
Into deer prints long gone.

Dangle bells,
Skating partners
Winking blue and yellow,
A new garden grows upon your
Simple throne
One of manufactured
Girth
One of old-time lace.

O Tannenbaum
Of pine crisp with firelight
Flickers,
The world is different now;
Not the place of brisk breezes
Rattling old antlers dropping
Red acid to fill the earth.

Somehow the ground has ceased
To bless bark
Yet still shall you glisten

To those old days of memory.

Ah pine queen
Rotting away as death claims
The soul
How bright your last spark has been.

December 24, 2015

NEVER AGAIN

We march,

Skin, bones, rags,

To looming gas

As ignorant as geese

Before a slaughter,

Starved petals

Of life

Doomed to the grace

Of almighty

Judge

And king.

May 5, 2016

WHERE GO
THE MEN OF PEACE

Where go the men of peace?

Where hide the women of hope?

For deep in this hollow

desert dust

where springs the blood

of bombs

the collateral damage

of innocents,

No one speaks for them.

No one speaks for

the red swept

children

swaddled in dust

after the bunkers come

crashing through.

No one

cries foul when

doctors die

deep in Gaia's bosom

broken and torn apart

by coward's toys.

Where lies the brave soul to speak

for these

creatures caught

by war?

September 28, 2016

HOW IS IT THAT THE BREEZE

How is it that the breeze

Flows

West

While I loiter

East

Of hell

That nook of madness

Where light filters down from a canopy

Of broken cedar boughs?

In olden days masts were built of such

fine trunks

To tame winds

And guide massive hulks

Across wave stressed ocean currents.

Ah! To see this place

Remote,

Docile,

Yellowing with frost fed

Mornings;

I feel this death approaching
Building into leaf lost twigs,
Fingers railing against
Currents.

Even ferns have fallen out with
Roots
Dry mulch
To feed silent earth,

While jay above sings
The last reveille to olden
Days
When trunks spawned green
And prayed to noon day sun;

When song
Flowed like rain
Waking cricket strings
And frog chants;

When flies flit

Seeking companionship with moose hair

And swatting tails.

East of hell,

This silent tomb awaits a new

Dulling coat

Warm for roots nestled beneath but

Cold and dead for those above.

November 15, 2016

THE FORLORN EARTH

Welcome home!
This windward plain greets
with stunted growth
broken branches, lost life.

Here the snow
comforts dead grass
with its cold embrace.

Strange how fallow the ground
has become
all the poplars strewn
like bodies desolate.

Here there are no
souls alive; not even robins
ring the bare bark with song.

I suppose
I should have expected

this from folly.

I should have guessed
that all it took was
the soundless
thrash of the bomb,
the powered
force tearing life
from the brutalized soil.

I should have thought
that once we entered the place
where the self-rightious
seldom leave,
where the main claim
is to meet God,
find heaven
seek Jesus
praise Allah
that we would soon lose our sense of self
our place among trolling ants
flippant fish, silent lynx.

I stopped seeking
such daft dens
full of fire, brimstone, and myrth for
I somehow knew
grass grew without
the force of God.

I knew
this dead land needed
no Satan to guide its
daily day.

I knew that under
guise of
power we
took beauty and scarred
its surface,
suffocated
its life
and left black rich earth
souless, broken,
empty.

Even the louse cannot

sleep beneath

torn branches

and broken bark.

How welcome

I feel

now that heaven is

but a forlorn soul

left to rot.

How smart we were

to master all

without thought.

How brilliant

to think that we were

sovereign masters

of this blue ball made black

who could carve new faces on

bashed rock.

All that granite, crystals baking

in sovereign sun, shine hollow
for no hand claims with curious
fingers.

Somehow I wish
we could lift lonesome
timbers back to green stands
restore queen white pine
and her subjects
to their proper place
turning these great blackened
granite hills once again into
richly carved statues.

April 2015

BARD

Four hundred years
Long
You have lain
Those careful strokes
Silent.

How can we forget
To utter
The charm of rogues
Witches, rabble?

Yes. You sang of love
Odes to wake nightingales at noon
From idle rest,
Brought princes to ruin
Shook ghosts from cobwebs
Deep in vaults.

I have heard Hamlet
Wandered angst driven

To sin against father
While Shylock stroked beard
Itching for his pound of flesh.

Ah! Old Lear,
Addled with loss, mad with guilt,
Thy fool kept you from storms
Quick strike
While Scottish MacBeth
Did fall broken and lost
Over the cradle that gold thrones offer.

Yes, silent you lie
Alongside Tomkins' glowing
Chant
Melted into the fabric

Time has left,
Stoking our souls
To find new coals
For old songs.

April 23, 2016

DEAR MISS COATES

By the time you see this I'll have gone
along the open road and tested the ferrets
of my soul. A sinner I have become, as
cruel a beast as any myth could create. A
soul so blemished by mistakes, the jacket
that surrounds tightens to cut the
circulation.

I should have tender mercies for my hair,
tender forgiveness for my heart, love for
my hands and breast.

I have neither. Just these empty promises,
hope squandered like gold. Save a word
and I could light a flame under my feet.

I'm alone with my shadow, alone with my
chair, sitting among the ruins of things
I've received, things I've taken for granted;
things I've hoped for. I've no photographs

of dead people, they walk through my life,

a dead creature among the dead.

I've left this note to say how sorry I feel

along the way, I hope that beyond the

grave, you are watching out for yourself

the way I never could.

Yours in the end
Jameson Kooper

Spring 1993

PHOTO OF THE HAPPY LOVER AT REST

In some room, where roses grow green
from chalk sills, the music has gone to
New Haven where I am not, where I never
was.

Only her eyes, chocolate ponds ringed in
cat tails are here, on solid paper, cold
dead for the trunk that grew to make it
has long since spread in dust on the pile
of a mill floor.

Her smile is stamped, the colour long
dried, the pink shine of her dress
betraying the white velvet and tan breast
beneath.

She is stamped, the sleeves and buttons
hiding the arm rivers, the falls of stringy
black bond plants directing towards her

wrists.

She is gone with only the faded wisp of
brown sheen stamped upon her brow. She
is gone and I am here to say
good bye.

1993

PEPSI CRUSH

I have become a ghost haunted by Pepsi
froth and Coke caffeine. I cannot even sit
with pen in palm without their demon
calls lilting down the steps of green to the
cool cellar door where they await the
Christmas rush.

How I wish they could play their songs on
cellar wood and leave me the calm among
words; or perhaps taunt a cellar lock to
speak in tongues to plastic wrappers, the
bags of chip pieces warming up to their
ghostly howls.

See how they tempt the Downy from its
lair among the cans of tomato soup.

If I am in limbo among the ghosts of
addict's flairs here at the table pen in
palm, can the attic above be the heaven

away from the Coke calls?

Perhaps they thrive up there in the cold of winter better than in the cellar below.

February 3, 1994

LOSING THE SCARLET LOVER

The foundering mast, the up-turned
planks of rot,
water sogged by the dock,
I knew her well as one closed book with its
beacon mark listing.

She was not the greatest of all steamers
that roamed ice waters
nor the good duchess of skies,
Hindenburg, her uncoupled hinges
scratching the cloth skin to bleed fire:
hydrogen collapsing the great bag into
ashes.

She was not an object of deck and sail
pulsating up and down upon
the seas, nor the reliable tug pulling
crippled metal giants home
the rope and chain maintaining the path
teased near the point of break.

A beacon she was though fog and haze of
evening made that light difficult to spot
before rocks collapsed rigging and deck
into puppet melt.

She was one instant on the water, the
glorious smile
of bow and stern, the deep chocolate
brown of rigging sturdy,
alive scarred by barnacles
stuck tight below water bright in the rays
of noon day sun.

I see her there, arched solid but broken
with sores of sea battles past.
I see her photo of moments and I pray that
masts can be repaired,
sturdier metal can replace wood rot;
that a new strong belly can grow and
catch waves with zeal,
casting out into the unknown beyond
harbor lights.

I hope that distant sun will shine and how
ripe and good she'll be
Although I cannot see beyond the point
with all its dusk this eve.

Only sol truly casts the crew.
Only sol in morning knows when dreams
end and wine is raised
against the bow in praise and glory.

1994

SEASONS

Seasons have passed
and I am not alive
like other jays
that flit among the
greenery.

Roosting by
the feeder gay
I pick not the delicious
seeds
sitting like glinting jewels.

I do not fly
forth from branch
to see the world.

I crow not for a mate
guide her to my bosom
so she can rest with me.

I have no eggs bearing my soul
no chicks bearing my imprint.

I am just this thing
caught on a branch
seated folly on display
blue and black feathers
courting wind.

I wish I could rise
awaken and break
this torpid phase that
cloaks.

But I sit
buffeted, the self
alone among the
opportune
watching them feast
and fight over the trough.

My soul stands still

I am watching history
pass leaving nary a mark
on its surly shell.

92

2001

ATIKOKAN STRIP MALL

Watching the dead lumber
bloated along white tiles
past white walls past
fluorescent lights
I do not see the mural
of townsmen building a town
but the masking of eroding
Floral Creations;

The weathered granite of a McTaggart's
sign,
going the way of the old Red and White,
once blossoming with apples and cereal
boxes now
a strip mall of Music city and
Exquisite.

There is a gaiety about the place,
stark wooden benches,
rubber plants donated to keep

appearances

rather like a marriage that has been

overwatered.

Only spooks in jeans roam halls, specters

in logos, malted hair,

the fellow in the corner

with his bottle of Coke,

the couple of elderly ladies ordering

in the Second Cup

sitting at tables

setting to memories of mines that

died the Dodo way.

Like most ghosts, they blend in the walls

well

the young yawn, floating in and out of

the Movie Hut

the last palace of leisure,

the sauna of the dead,

the last house God visits before Satan

absorbs the lot and parking.

April 4, 2002

HASHEM

I look to you
to hold me now,
your bronzed arms
warm,
cradling;
for I dread what future
brings
lying here
hospital bound
bloodied by wayward heartbeats
that refuse to convert
to normalcy.
I know where that path leads.

I know you wait with crossed arms
at the rainbow's end
to judge a poor excuse
of flesh.

That is after all what you are:

supreme court and final appeal
to clemency.

But I also know there can be solace in
your hardened look and kindly hands.
Did you not create us out of love
not judgment?

So hold me now
until the time.
Hold me please rather than
coldly stare on.

May 26, 2008

HASHEM 2

The savage
beast you have become.
I recognize nothing of the good
others claim for you.

Perhaps if I bowed in supplication
at your coattails you might
fathom some kindness,
even sit with me on those rough nights
when the gale bends the boughs outside.

But I am too proud
to give in to your
soldier's beats,
your savage ways,
your duplicitous gaze.

I know better than
to follow a slinking tiger
as it presses upon prey.

October 28, 2013

DAD

Dad:

With day passed
I try to coax memory
from dry ashes.
Listless, we piece pieces
sort through a tangle of life you left us.

"Can't buy those things" while
the din plays for audio tape,
"a mean little girl" as he sweeps
up the pot trouncing all comers
twinkling pupils even as stinging death
rises to greet you from hospital bed.

What a mess of love left dangling for us to
grasp.
But each time we see the reclining figure
seated among branches of a cabin long
gone

or look into those stilled eyes captured
briefly by camera lens
We shall remember how lively
a spirit that resided, how gentle into that
good night
you rode; the tangle rejuvenated as a web
that captures
lunar glow.

Dad

We feel space, see empty chair wood
listless, lurking by the table seeking
sustenance from your
frail surly frame.

We see ashen skin, stolen sight, broken
breath
but feel love in a house cut and built,
sturdy shelves to keep books in,
night light to spurn shadows.

Ah me! You surround us with loving

hands

though they remain still and quiet beneath

coffin wood.

In sleep we listless souls will find you

again for from memory

comes new light, new direction.

January 22, 2015

THE FIRST SNOW

Dad:

The first snow is upon the grass.
Five they say enough to blanket
your bed beautifully I think.
You probably wouldn't know
sleeping so soundly as you do.

You were always deep when night
was upon us, letting out those loud
roars that wake bears from dens.

Yes. A forest echo,
A jack pine moaning to cover
the tracks you left of past days
when green was your pleasure
and wind pain.

I remember those days well, building up
work shop spires to rival Everest.

Ah you never slept then,
driving from one ache to
another masking with silence
as nature turned time towards
night.

I miss you now as I look over pink stone
peeking from white.

Quite peaceful isn't it,
the white blanket slowly resting
to warm the earth
covering pines deep
mounting holes where sleeping things
lie.

Quiet, warm, safe. You never had it so
good.

December 2015

COLD

Cold,
The pallor greyish, ashen
the lips open but no warm
breeze blows;

The cold sweat of
illness has fallen away
to the silent
sting of death.

Eyes stolid,
their flinching has
long since been
extinguished
in the slow
shutting up
of senses.

Cold, hands no longer
claim the itch that

streaks long

nasal crest.

No. Peace

has found a harbour

The Universe,

has

come to earthly roots

and picked its sullen

soul up from out

of the crumpled form.

He rests where I cannot

follow.

He will sleep well tonight.

January 21, 2015

DEAR DEATH

Dear Death:

Why do you play so?
Grisly beast!
Some of us do like
To admire this blue-green
Marble
Shining by sun's gay light.
Some might think you a jealous green
that we can look
Above while you reside below,
Grime and grit.
You are un-bowed by our
Weightless trifle,
Staring out upon the dark
Matter scattered like confetti about us.

April 2015

THE PREDATOR

Eyes

that stare

break the black and white world.

I should fear

the predator

preparing

its strike.

I should

stare back,

break those pupils

down to

constituent parts:

lens lying,

waiting my move,

testing the scent,

tasting the air.

I should fear the reaper

as he brings

his claws to bear
those tearing shearing
things that rip bellies
open.

But silence is his majesty.
His paws barely touch
snow as he closes
distance,
closes upon my
broken frame
sensing I am weak after all.

He should be afraid.
Mauling human flesh comes with
costs,
A few pounds of buckshot
will riddle his sleek
frame should he
complete his task.

Yet God guides
as he slices air forth,
breaking the swath

of birch to land,

glancing,

tearing at skin,

gripping the wind

and shutting down

life.

For the briefest

moment hunger claims

the beast and all else

is madness.

For the briefest of moments

he is sated,

struggling

but sated,

till the next call

comes,

till the next

prey meets

a grisly end.

April 2015

DEATH

I feel you
coming,
old man,
that scythe
sharp.

I hear it takes
but a second
and wind is knocked
dead.

I hear chess is your choice
of sport
along sandy beaches
black to white.

I play poor
so I do not expect much
but you knew that
to begin with.

I hear

no escape

can come from

a god like you,

underworld master,

king of silence.

I hear sleepless,

you are the wanderer

supreme.

Even antelope

cannot race

away for you

cut down

trees easily without

end.

Tireless, you

will not stop until,

quota filled

we follow

to your humble home,

King of slumber,
restless bed.

We think that once
laid to earthly rest
all is done.

But we know not
what lies beyond
your veil
which fear brings
sallow ground.

We hope,
gladsome space
full with flowers,
bees and scented
breeze will greet.

We shake
to see fire
rife, rankled
gown of soot laid

upon every tree
and bauble,
the screams masking
fun to come.

I know you come
old man
scythe drawn
sharp.

Underworld king,
I know you are
waiting to fill
another line.

I hear
you take all
and leave no wind
to waken new
trees.

I fear nothing
for

I know rest is just
another word for work.

April 2015

THE SILENCE OF WINTER

Pink stone peeks from white shine
defiant, as if to stand and deliver.

Ah the cold crown becomes you old
fellow
you who calmly slept in chair silent.

A whole year
passed like wind I think. Yet stolid
you sit on your throne
visiting worm subjects and ant pests.

I hear down there it is just as warm as
above
but tell no lies I do not wish
to prove doubters wrong.

Mom has found solace, sure and
steady like blue falls,
though her eyes

betray the silence of kitchen
chores.

She feels
brief tears silent inspection
of old news.

Ah, you would think your voice has been
cut short but down among reels
I have found new songs
of old days to remind of the way home.

April 2015

THE FINAL RESTING SPACE

Ah!
Here lies they say
The final resting space,
The quiet mourning hole
Where we lay our trees to grow new roots
Where new lives find new needles to
Catch sun.

I hear this land of white pine proud
Is a homeland for muskrat pure
Working with beaver to build
New dams to keep water.

Strange bedfellows, they patch
The roof and keep the needle path
Fresh
So pines can resonate with glow
As life grows full
And fast.

Final quiet watering hole,
This shimmering place should vibrate
The death of thousands,
The collapse of races
Born and bred to murder each other in the
Name of God.

Yet this mourning hole has found worms,
Fat and full,
Feasted by robins quick to catch
That pink flesh slinking.

Yes you would not know that life blood
Drew this land full with death:
Scattered arms, legs, torsos of another
year

When climate change resounded,
Fear trampled lives under foot,

When oceans sank islands
And guns roared answer.

Now look at this land

Fresh as mist.

There are loon calls beckoning the
Crows from their lairs,
Frog song cooing the air
With love.

You wouldn't think fear had died
To find new days from tattered earth.

December 11, 2015

LONG YOU HAVE GONE

Long you have gone
Soft spoken soul
To lie with gods.

Far from here
Among fields of snow
I know you rest

At peace while we
Look on
Remembering.

December 31, 2015

MEMORANDUM

Memorandum to

Henry Theodorus Kooper Jr.

(Sept. 21, 1922 – Jan. 22, 2015):

Silent stand

The pine grove,

Needles singing an aching moan.

Below trunks

The pink stone lays

Reminding all

The soul that made once merry.

Ah to think time has sped

Summer green to

Winter white;

Yet close we are to thee.

I still feel cold forehead nestled

Like a precious jewel in shaking

Arms welcoming new,
Decrying old.

Deer footfalls declare visitors
From pine den as we stand,
Stones before thee.

How well you sleep while we go on
Your soft whisper frame but memory
Your quiet soul listening
In oaken chair, the living room of
distance.

Squirrels seeking cones in break-neck
Trails fail to dull
Relentless rest
Nor disturb calm
That snow drifts bring

While we
Silent watchers
Stand to mourn
Like stones in a row.
January 14, 2016

IV

FINDING MY WAY
BACK TO THE LIGHT

SPRIGS

Sprigs,
We were the
Tender shoots
Grasping the first rays,

Glinting dew awakening
The potential that comes to
Tamarack roots and spruce
Green.

We were kings
Of the undergrowth,
Picking our way up the
Path past
Older fatter bushes
And twigs,

Breaking to reach canopy
Above where robins
Regaled

Tales of worms nipped
And slugs dropped.

How I remember the west gale
Twisting when lightning flushed
The ground smoking and tore
At our woody stems
Washing wet the rains of yesteryear.

We stand now
Towering over rivers flushed with froth
Ground saturated with shadow
Where new shoots
Break fertile soil.

October 28, 2016

HASHEM (GOD)

I look aloft
To see milky arms
Embracing warmth
Against the dark
Threatening
To tear each
Flare apart.

I have heard it said
Light
Broke blank
Canvas
Open,

Spread colour like
Melting ice
Across flat
Window sill
Dripping a world alive,

Springing life

From mud

And turning cloudless ocean

Into busy

Buffet of jellies and crab,

Tuna and shark.

Yes I hear it said

Light

Fed the land

Turning riverside green

And feeding deer and bear,

Wolf and raven alike.

Yet I look to galaxy arms glowing

And see

None of that;

Just dusty glimmering

Of ancient suns

Erecting grand cosmic

Storms

That here

Make northern lights.

Yet this broad
Canvas must house
Other sharks,
Other deer
Distant,
Fed in light.

Somewhere, lichens
Break down
Rock and shoots push
Through to pray
To Aten's glinting jewel
Light-years away.

Somewhere another sill
Frames the day
And holds the dark at bay.

November 28, 2016

LETTER RUMINATIONS FROM THE COVERS

Mary Beth:

When I, alone with my song wanders
across the valley of white pine tall

I see two chocolate bubbling pools melting
me into rain puddles that robins like to sip
upon.

When I, along with my sheet wanders
through the rain forest scent below pine
needles,

I see your smile break like rainbow rays
through the boughs warming my cheek
with its touch.

When I alone with the pockmarked ceiling
wanders past the dew of spider's silk on

prune roots,

I hear your meadow lark's sweet song
whisper delight that day has come.

1994

DEAR SANDRA:

I came home to the land of memory
to find the house vacant
the rooms cold to touch. Their colours
faded,
the red of angry outbursts are dulled
somewhat by the bitter retort of change.

The faces that reside here are no longer
mirrors of joker's smiles, no longer
prodding the insults and I do not know
what to do.

The greens are brighter than ever here, the
blues pale frame the windows out of which
I see the tribal chants of tourists from that
far-away land, taunting in echoes.

I do not know what to do; perhaps
approach a Martian from Kuzbain,
or snigger and weep at the folly of the

strange glasses I wore,
the playgrounds where child's play was
sanctioned anger and frivolity.

Faces have changed, the house of cards
stands stolid, old, the last calls from
wounded dogs of old.

I want so much to throw the windows
open,
let the new breezes collect around the
foundation,
sweep the jokers and queens like a twister
to Oz where they can kill witches.

Leave me the greens and the blues,
the sky and the trees,
the architect's plans for the preserve of old
growth forest with its pines and firs,
poplars and spruce.

Let the granite of life, the soil of youth
remain like opened Coke bubbling and

frothy.

Perhaps we can talk we two
again about Dick Francis.
I would like to connect.

Yours truly,
Jameson Kooper

November 27, 1993

SONG TO GEORGE

The other day
I found you again
a Bermuda colour splashed
against the blue. Those shades
like your guitar was cool enough!

You were the quiet one
but your smile flashed
a chameleon before my ears
for you never sounded so confident.

You even had time to remember those
fab roots
among the album pickings
a recognition of an awful truth:

you were a Beatle
among those incredulous kids,
bright and rooted to earth
among Ravi's children.

1999 – October 28, 2013

I DIDN'T HAVE AN ACE

I

didn't have

an ace in the hole

back when moon men walked

and dinosaurs clunked from

meal to meal.

Back when I was

king of reptiles

and Major Matt on his sled

traipsing the lunar land

crater to crater

weaving wind patterns others could not

see.

They all thought he's nuts,

strange,

stranger on a pole

later gay.

I was a noisy

crow
at times
perched from that dismal
place
that no one
could figure
upon,
sometimes comfortable,
at others restless
and uncertain.

Yet in that place
I learned to tend
a future as brittle
as wax candles.

I never became the politician
or the actor.
I became the cook,
the inserter,
the teacher, the coach.
I became the teller
of yarns

that drew bated
breath from
little wee eyes.

I wandered in the dark
at times lost,
at times welcoming of death's cold
clasp
and persisted somehow
moving forward
one clumsy step
at a time:
learning the length,
feeling the fabric,
realizing me.

I have long left my lunar sled,
my dinosaur crawl
in vapors past
long left my crow's perch for
the mire of daily trial.

Yet I knew myself

better than
I realized
back when.

It's cool
to feel
comfortable in your own
skin.

October 26, 2011

SIM

I controlled her black hair,
created her from the database clay
and wrenched a rib to make
her man,
a dumb farthing wandering through a
glass life.

Shiny and new, I controlled her pee
made a house a gigabytes long,
small on furniture.
She went
from day to day to some hidden place,
a car beaten by dust shouted her away.

I controlled
her feast at Chanukah.
Hell she could even
be a criminal mind given my sense of
touch.

Yet, now, day to day

she goes

home dancing to music I choose,

calling a party over,

greening the jewel above

so that she can carry on

another day in peace.

Leave and for one

minute her world

comes apart,

tears shed

she yells obscenities skyward

as if it matters,

refuses chores and piddles

in every corner, the pissed

cat demanding

better hands.

I admit the pleasure

of seeing her crumble into a

broken heap when left

lacking sleep.

I love playing at

cupid bringing her love and
lust and a snoggle in bed.

When
she becomes ghost I choose her
grandiose return and what will follow
forth.

Ah God!
I can see why you worked
your hands upon clay
to build up creatures that call you
their own.

How much pleasure you must have
tormenting the savages,
breaking them like branches
relieving them of pleasure
busting their lives.

How brave we are facing the likes
of you.

October 28, 2013

FORWARDS

Today
I begin as always
Trodden, twisting
Twirling, always fleeing back
Always meeting forwards,
with each tree
And rock and hill placed
Perfect.
Each moment is readied perfect
Like God.

Then back
To before
I whirl
A furious top
All piss and wind
Going nowhere.

Strange to see
As I begin again

Mounting new rocks and pines and prairie

Wheat

Hoping once more to break tradition;

Train my soul

To work new wonders.

But forwards I fall

Into that backward

Space from which I spawned.

Trivial it seems

Rushing backwards so forwards

I see

And yet alone I spark towards

A backward place

Where wind is king

And I am slave.

Forwards I begin

This treacherous road

Full with suicide march

And sugar rush,

Slave still to whims of time

Though careful

Not to let the dew settle
And grass grey brown.

Ah me,
Wretch to whimsy
Time continues to fold my soul
Though backwards I spiral
Looking forwards.

Ah me,
Slave to death,
Supreme commander of all flocks,
I see backwards
To grazing days,
When life was simple,
Amoeba stuff,
Those slow forward arms
Enveloping dark.

Forwards I begin
Seeming stuck to tradition
Certain that somehow
I will find my path with seeds

To grow better lives from.

Ah! Forwards I begin
Hoping this time
I see light
Rather than that darkening
Dusk where all life sleeps
Soundly on,
Skipping wind.

December 29, 2015

NEW YEAR'S GRAVEYARD

Grey passing for blue,
Silent grass blanketed
As pine moans
Comment on
Finality.

Resting I suppose,
this stone, pink,
a marker to past woes
and grateful memories,
stands
Against drab day.

I know you sleep soundly,
home of peace,
calm of night,
As old brings new,
weathering one hour
Further.

I often think what it must be
Like, that cold space where
Even the worms flee;

Marked
To remind of footfalls
Long past due.

Numbers tell different tales
"1922" broken like vinyl,

Shattered,

Not much different than now:
"2015", full of death and blood
Meaning nothing.

You sleep better I assume Than I
trapped by deer prints daily on.

A buck should stop to graze
Upon the hidden shoots
Seek that last fresh light
Of older ghosts.

He is beautiful to see

Brown eyes, dignity

Lifted upon a sleek frame.

Careful,

Ready,

Brave,

A king of pine trunks

And snow squalls,

Toughest part of winter.

Yet he graces your temple

Leaves a reminder

Of future fertile

Days

When beetles

Will crawl busy upon your throne.

Pink marks the past

So well

As yonder year break

Upon the stone strewn sea.

Wake now to see the
Wonders of this world.
Wake to see what
Life chooses to miss.
Wake from the night
So bleak
To chance upon warm
Breeze brought softly.
Wake to see how warm spring shall
Be
When silent grass grows tall
Glowing alive!

December 31, 2015

PRAIRIE WINDS

Where wheat
Once flowed
Like ocean waves
I see endless sky
To horizon break.
Somewhere east,
I cannot see that
Lakes prosper
And pine groves
Stand
Flush with green.

I imagine
How they greet
Prairie breeze
Warm with spring
Pluck.

Do they welcome
Western bounty

With open

Needles

Relishing fruit from God?

Do they welcome

The song

Of flax sprout

And coyote call?

Are they ready to

Sing songs back

Of loon nests

And deer rustle?

Do they send their love

Wrapped in God's glow?

December 6, 2016

WHITE SPRUCE SONG

He is an old friend to me

Long and stretched thin

Not like others

So fat and short

Behind shed boards

And ladders

Of olden days.

No! He is a tall

Stately green

Rising to catch

Poplar leaves

And pine swath.

I wonder how this

King should

Find his way through

The long

Weary

Blizzards

And twisting

Winds of ancient storms

To find solace

In this quiet before

Dawn.

How does outstretched

Branch

Greet hazy light

When others have fallen

Before the might of God?

How does

He make peace with space?

December 7, 2016

THE CALM WATER

Finally,
I have found you,
This quiet place
Where mirror green
Washes calm shores.

Yes,
Supple waves do break
Brief
To say
That blue space
Is alive
With breeze.

Barely caressing,
This warm wind
Shakes
Some pine loose
As if to say
I own these branches.

Yet, at

Lake side, look

To see

a mirror of sky,

Regal spruce

Ancient granite grey,

The majesty of creator

Painted upon calm water

Here God is smiling.

Here I find peace at last.

December 7, 2016

WHITE OTTER CASTLE

You fit snug

Among

Trunks shaded in pine needle,

ancient domain

Of quiet dream

And broken promise.

I hear she never came,

Never saw this

Log Throne

Of Scottish

Hands,

A wild fortress

Nestled far from prying eyes

Where only loons

Sing

Songs to soothe

Spirit.

I hear wolves and deer

Visit quickly,

Still suspecting
Somewhere
Human
Hands are stirring.

But silence is a bitter
Teacher
For
Only red pine
Moan the
Tears of
Wood
Decaying.

Only spruce
Spin tales
Of love lost and death won.

December 7, 2016

FRENCH RIVER SPRING

Tender shoots
Rise to feast upon Aten's
Gold, breaking soil
Long held in winter blanket.

With each dew day, glinting
Jewels wake a sleepy world,
Shaking spiders from cobwebs,
Ants from dens,
As light brings life new fruit.

Soon a canopy above will
Shelter a shadow world
Of deer and wolf,
Fox and bear,
As rapids regale
Upon rocks those frosty days that winter
Tracked and
Spring fresh days to come.

I hear this place

Dressed in white spruce fine

And white pine grace

Has seen these musky

Mornings many a year

From sapling to ancient root.

Ah how warm this breeze embraces.

How warm God's hand can be

Upon a hill once ravaged by

Sleet and snow.

Only brackish ice by quiet pool

Recalls the bitter blizzard that

Once called rock home.

November 2005

COMPLETE LIST
OF POEMS

I LIGHT

IV FINDING MY WAY BACK TO THE LIGHT

ABOUT THE AUTHOR

Jameson Kooper was born in 1963. Writing had always occupied his youth but it wasn't until he was enrolled in a creative writing class at Lakehead University that he began to hone his craft in 1992. He was subsequently published in the Lakehead's creative writing journal, The Ventriloquist in 1993. For a period of 13 years, he lived in Brandon, Manitoba returning to Atikokan, his birthplace, in 2013 to help support his aging parents. His father's death in 2015 influenced him into writing and initially publishing his work on Facebook until recently when Mischievous Books published his first chapbook of poetry. When he is not writing, Jameson is very busy singing at local town jams, doing voice over work for Voices.com, writing songs, or just sitting enjoying his favourite series Doctor Who.